Sports Page

Sports Page

Ken Waldman

LITERARY PRESS
LAMAR UNIVERSITY

ISBN: 978-1-942956-75-4
Library of Congress Control Number: 2019957567

Printed in the USA

Lamar University Literary Press
Beaumont, Texas

For my late father, Albert Waldman, big sports fan; and for my sister, Lisa, my brother-in-law, Hal, and my nieces, Rachel and Melissa, also big sports fans, and strong supporters of my work

Recent Poetry from Lamar University Literary Press

Bobby Aldridge, *An Affair of the Stilled Heart*
Walter Bargen, *My Other Mother's Red Mercedes*
Mark Busby, *Through Our Times*
Julie Chappell, *Mad Habits of a Life*
Stan Crawford, *Resisting Gravity*
Chip Dameron, *Waiting for an Etcher*
Glover Davis, *My Cap of Darkness*
William Virgil Davis, *The Bones Poems*
Jeffrey DeLotto, *Voices Writ in Sand*
Chris Ellery, *Elder Tree*
Dede Fox, *On Wings of Silence*
Alan Gann, *That's Entertainment*
Larry Griffin, *Cedar Plums*
Michelle Hartman, *Irony and Irrelevance*
Katherine Hoerth, *Goddess Wears Cowboy Boots*
Michael Jennings, *Crossings: A Record of Travel*
Gretchen Johnson, *A Trip Through Downer, Minnesota*
Ulf Kirchdorfer, *Chewing Green Leaves*
Jim McGarrah, *A Balancing Act*
J. Pittman McGehee, *Nod of Knowing*
Laurence Musgrove, *Bluebonnet Sutras*
Laurence Musgrove, *One Kind of Recording*
Benjamin Myers, *Black Sunday*
Godspower Oboido, *Wandering Feet on Pebbled Shores*
Carol Coffee Reposa, *Underground Musicians*
Jan Seale, *The Parkinson Poems*
Steven Schroeder, *the moon, not the finger, pointing*
Glen Sorestad, *Hazards of Eden*
Vincent Spina, *The Sumptuous Hills of Gulfport*
W.K. Stratton, *Ranchero Ford/ Dying in Red Dirt Country*
Wally Swist, *Invocation*
Loretta Diane Walker, *Desert Light*
Loretta Diane Walker, *Ode to My Mother's Voice*
Dan Williams, *Past Purgatory, a Distant Paradise*
Jonas Zdanys, *Three White Horses*

For information on these and other Lamar University Literary Press books go to www.Lamar.edu/literarypress

Acknowledgments

I am grateful to the editors of the following journals in which some of these poems, or versions of these poems, first appeared:

Aethlon
Asheville Poetry Review
Asspants
Cobalt Review
Connecticut River Review
Cold Mountain Review
Convolvulus
Elysian Fields Quarterly
Eratica
Free Lunch
Green Hills Literary Lantern
High Plains Literary Review
Intentional Walk
Lactuca
Listening Eye
The MacGuffin
Nerve Cowboy
Onionhead
Piedmont Literary Review
Poetpourri
Pudding
Redneck Review
Sidewalks
South Dakota Review
Southern Poetry Review
Tar River Poetry
Yet Another Small Magazine

CONTENTS

Father's Day, 2018

I

II

III

VI

VII

Father's Day, 2018

Though you're seven years gone,
I thank you today for making time
to play games when I was a boy.
I'm happy to remember how
you taught me to throw
a spiral, dig up a short hop,
breathe deeply and bounce the ball
exactly three times before foul shots.
Later you taught me how to drive
a stick, grill a burger, balance
a checkbook. You cheered
my every victory, railed
at my shortcomings.
Dad, you taught me to be
your son, competitor.

I

Baseball Man

Drafted, signed, paid, groomed, called up,
sent down, called up, sent down,
reassigned, traded, traded, traded,
released, re-signed, a dozen towns,
leagues, a dozen years, a whirl
of county seats, blighted fields,
bad teams, women, humidity
and heat, thirty-one years old,
sore shoulder and back, a hummer
that won't, divorced, veteran
of suitcase, bus, beer, asked to coach,
carefully extends a big right hand,
shakes, sold to the organization,
this time for life.

The Punt Returner

Scorning fair catch,
helmet gleaming gold
in the sun, he side-
steps one tackle,
quickly lateral cuts
to break another,
veers outside, picks
blocks toward sideline,
tightropes past midfield,
the forty-five, the forty,
is shoved out intact,
his Olympian nine-second,
twenty-four-yard dash:
no fumble, no flag,
no punt returner
lying broken and inert
on hard artificial turf.

The Whiz

Sophomore year, Ozzie blossomed into
The Whiz. Part Magic, part Bird,
a 6 foot 6 leaper whose heady
playmaking sparked the break, he'd sneak
behind-the-back bounce passes
for slam-bang jams, or snake past
helpless arms for his own cool two.

The next Jordan, one pro scout said.
Worth ten million, said an agent,
jostling to get in a word.
Both missed a certain Ms. Farmer,
a tall, pretty tutor who taught
a struggling redshirt to write with heart—
and hooked the star his freshman fall.

After a junior year wedding, a wife
who needed tending slowed Ozzie's
all-court game, and he slipped
from top draftee to B.A. in English,
a minor in History. The second-guess:
married too young, school too consuming,
The Whiz dissed a rare, big-money gift.

Skyway Lanes

God is bowling. Pins in place,
he stands erect, twenty feet behind
the line, toes touching the tips
of rented, green-laced bowling shoes.
Raising the ball chest-high,
three right hand fingers wiggling
inside the black ball's holes,
his left hand spreads under hard rubber.
When the grip fits just right,
he weighs the ball like a scientist-general
hefting a bomb.

God has memorized Don Carter's advice
to bowlers. Before each frame,
breathing like a weightlifter
preparing to lift, he shuts his eyes
and visualizes the perfect throw:
four-step approach, smooth slide,
controlled release, follow-through
with right hand reaching, making the ball
skid, then roll, then hook across pinewood
to hit the 1-3 pocket, ten pins toppling
like ten thousand.

God is ready.

The Hustler

End of game, cue
kissing cushion,
the hustler chooses
spin for protection
against a scratch,
catches the eight
just right, watches
the ball fall straight
in the side, thunk
like bone knocking rock,
a sound that talks
like his rich doctor
uncle, top pool shark
who taught the boy
not to rush, but work
a table, run it slowly,
play like making love,
because love was money.

Salter's Funeral

Tuesday, the funeral, and I remember
Saturday, and Salter's last round,
a 78. Salter bought the burgers,
fries, beers and we replayed his chip on six
to save par, his drive on nine, the three iron
from behind a tree on thirteen,
his wedge from the trap—a buried lie—
on fifteen, his tricky downhill
putt on sixteen. Salter, then me.

God knows, why at home, indoors
before a lousy TV ballgame,
waiting before dinner. Salter must have groaned
at the wrongness, like a shank, because
it should have been on eighteen, Salter,
sandy-haired at fifty, boyish Salter smiling
as he waggled his driver, pivoting—
that slash of a swing—to crack the ball 270,
Salter, no more than a full six iron
to the green, wisecracking, striding down
that fairway, golf glove flapping in his pocket,
caddie following respectfully, Salter, pumped,
seeing me drill a sweet four iron
to within fifteen feet, choosing
the seven instead, hitting, a huge divot,
and the ball's right at the stick,
digs, rolls, some spin, and it lips
the cup. It should have been
on eighteen, Salter knowing how close,
just how close, to an eagle, one foot
on the green, one foot still in the fringe,
chuckling to himself—a tap-in bird,
a 78—with me beside him,
telling him how good he'd been all along,
when he clutched his chest, and went.

Wheelchair Tennis

They had to have been family: a man
feeding backhands to a woman in the chair
a few feet in front of the baseline,

making her strain shoulders and arms
for each ball, which she'd strike
first cross-court, then down-the-line

with a steady grim accuracy born
from a lifetime of smacking two-handers
relentlessly, competitively,

both adults now turning to the girls
dressed in white, mama's little legs,
poised by the net to collect the misses.

Barb's Tennis Camp

A warmer child might have cried
fearing leaving home
for a month, first time ever.

Barb turned her back,
didn't watch them drive away,
then clutched her racket,

gripped it as she'd been taught,
raced to the courts. Boys
and girls her age and older

seemed everywhere. She climbed
some bleachers, took in
the action, watched kids hit.

Her clean face caught
bright sun like a flat slap
forehand: dad's usual reproach.

Metronomic

Downstairs, his sister
practices badly, this
his punishment for not
being good enough
to have made the squad,
and having no friends
to visit after school.
First Chopin, then Bach,
but getting them wrong.
Missed low notes, each
like their father, the way
that man argued long
and hard. Cracked
high notes, each
like their mother, nagging
in misplaced frustration.
Sick of sounding like this
when he was her age,
the boy took up sports.

Colossally bored, he slips
beneath sheets, naps,
and dreams of a key turning
a lock, perimeter jumpers
going swish, swish, swish,
days passing with a click.

Wrestling Lesson

Says coach:
To grow stronger

a wrestler has
got to grow more

flexible. More
than muscles, strength

is brains. Not
brawn. A little technical

agility is key.
That's it. I mean

you don't have to
pin, just win.

The Twins

Innocent-looking and polite, the boys
passed as happy-go-lucky angels.
If the teachers only knew. Ignored
by a father always busy at work,
saddled with a mother who allowed
free rein, the boys' mischief
escalated by degree: slashing tires,
torturing stray cats, bullying
eighth-graders, mugging a handicapped man.
Anything for a thrill. Anything.

Rich, the clever sharpshooting guard,
eventually won a basketball scholarship
to State. Ron, a half-inch shorter,
full-second slower, foul-prone,
got caught one night, landed in jail.
According to the court psychologist,
Ron was set up by his brother.
According to the high school coach,
the look-alikes shadowed one another.
According to the parents, why bother.

II

How Basketball Came to the Villages

I

Sun and snowball started
to fight. Would snowball
melt? Would the sun
freeze? God, preferring
a more civilized conflict,
invented the basketball.

II

Children everywhere
asked their parents:
*what are the dimply
skins that can't breathe,
aren't rocks, don't smell
like food, bounce good?*

III

When the whites came,
they saw leather balls
like arctic pumpkins.
Places to build gyms
with hoops at both ends,
new scoreboards, schools.

February Full Moon, Nome

After the city razed the old
hulking two-story wooden junker
kitty-corner to me, and sprayed
the graded lot, I sat watching
little kids slip like seal pups
as they slid flailing across
shiny wind-scoured ice, taking
the subzero cold to the bone.

Past midnight, a last teenager
gone, I laced long-unused skates,
wobbled to the makeshift rink.
Over and over I circled alone,
my stiff and imperfect ovals
like that insistent winter moon's
bright sixteen-hour orbit,
a frozen, warped halo.

Darts

Lowbrow barroom sport of beer
and smoke, the throw's quick flip
of wrist is a burnt-out cop
shooting his pointed shit
at the never-ending in-basket
across the desk; a secretary
sticking pins in her boss's face;
a tournament-tough husband and wife
glaring at a rare choked miss,
their high-school kids home
drunk on frozen daiquiris,
cutting the liquor with dope.

Nome Ballplayer

The Breaker Bar's newest lost fixture,
the King Islander, Skip, hoisted a bottleneck
which he tipsily drained, then banged
the counter for another. Forty pounds over
game-day weight, this broken young Eskimo
redneck, ex-Nome Beltz High three-sport prince,
now ran on chewing tobacco, beer,
the endless replay of mid-February
junior year high jinks: Valentine Friday,
the night he scored twenty-six; screwing
Teresa, the sauna at Luke's; the unlucky
slip on sidewalk ice, almost dodging
a skidding big-tired Chevy pickup
that never honked. *And gimme a double-shot
of Wild Turkey.* The memory of
being run over, pinned, losing ankle
and foot, left leg crushed at the calf.

A Run at the Shore

Last evening, watching a rose sunset
spread over ocean, I misstepped,
and fell with this sudden insight:
what almost broke . . . didn't.
The next moment—nothing
but a thud. And then I felt
my chin in wet, gravelly dirt,
my mouth full of gritty mud.
I pushed up, put what weight
I could on my sprained right ankle,
and glared at swollen seas,
at a blushing laughing sky
that said: I love you, my friend,
but *slow down*.
                        Hobbling,
to the road, shaking my head,
I rested often, testing the ankle.
So what, I thought, glancing west
at a bruised and watery horizon.
So I'd make it home after dark,
then shower and change. Always,
the same message. Always,
something out to get me.

Fat Girl on Ice

Ankles tight in laced white skates,
large body swathed in overalls,
she pushes off with the right,
glides the pond's width, sliding
easy as a sled. Forwards, backwards,
a well-executed one-legged pirouette
that spirals to blade-flashing
ballet grace. If the ice mirrored
the heart, she'd gaze down at a swan.

Yo fatso, you'll be goalie nothing
could ever get by you, a boy shouts,
leading several helmeted stick-handlers
to the ice. Sailing into the wind,
the fat girl quickly weaves, whizzes
like a left wing to steal a stick
from one boy, a puck from another,
winds up for an extra-weighted slapshot
aimed at the defenseman's teeth.

The Shooting Lesson

Deep in the woods you take me shooting.
You set the can on a tree trunk
and give me the pistol. Second try
I hit the metal straight on—

a heart shot, you tell me.
Then you grab the pistol
and cock it as you spot a squirrel
up a distant tree limb. You shoot
and miss. *Fucking squirrel*, you say,
cocking the pistol again, firing—

and then you keep doing it, cocking it
and firing bullets through leaves.
Reloading the pistol, you notice a rabbit
on spruce needles a few feet away.
You sight and shoot. The rabbit falls—
a heart shot.

You shoot the rabbit again.
We walk towards it. You tell me
you'll teach me how to butcher it
once we get home.

Fly Fishing the Chena

Knee-deep in river
he casts, the current
carrying the line

slowly downstream
to a green-black oval
of air bubbles,

grayling beneath.
The sun's going.
The big hill west,

still snowcapped,
shades the spot.
He tugs his hipboot tops

twice for luck.
With a flick he recasts
short. He reels, then jerks,

more wrist, this time
beyond the grayling hole
onto the one stripe of light.

In a second, a bite.
He plays the fish,
letting it run once,

then again, rod taut
from the weight's pull.
The next hours

establish the pact:
he reels, unhooks, cleans,
cooks, and eats the fish;

he lingers by the dying fire,
burying the bones; under
spruce he dreams of the fish

turned mermaid turned girl.

Tennis Pro, Juneau

Variable wind, mist, drizzle.
Occasional downpour. Rare sun.
Juneau weather. Everyday
but Monday a thirteen mile
commute. He parks, slings
tennis bag over a shoulder,
slams the car door, thinks

the gray sky gives away nothing:
the goddamn lot's a litter
of wadded candy wrappers,
crushed beer cans—beautiful;
nobody parks within lines—
so what vehicles get blocked;
the dumpster's as obvious

as the row of young spruce—
someone's lazy mistake;
the club's an ugly box—
perfect for this, the dead
part of town, a glacier
valley developed
into a southeast Alaskan

Levittown. He shuffles
up the steps. The time's
9:54 or 1:26. The month's
August or March. Clouds.
55°. Pushing open the door,
he smells sweat, something
sulfur-like. The weights

of the nautilus clank,
shoes on racquetball courts
squeak, the cash drawer
rings open. The echoing

thwock of tennis balls
make him think of muffled
rifle fire, his lifelong

loneliness, an asylum. Why
do people want to learn
tennis in Alaska? Why
is he the one teaching?
Tina, whose bright smile
he can't trust, asks
about today's lesson.

They start now, he says.
And strides past, toward
the locker room to change.

Alaska's Second Most Dangerous Sport

Riskier than commercial crabbing,
or biking the Anchorage flats
in traffic, or hunting bear, seal,
caribou, whale. Or trapping fox,
wolf, wolverine, lynx. Or driving
into a moose. Or boating when drunk.
Or falling too far into a mad
glacial wilderness. Riskier still
is the plane crash. Mine, moments
after hitting a hill, bleeding
from head wounds that would need
one hundred stitches to close,
suffering a concussion that would take
more than twenty months to heal,
I looked to my pilot, who allowed
he'd seen a dozen hockey injuries
that looked more severe.

Red Lantern

Behind front-runners breaking rail from Skwentna to Iditarod,
    northern lights like the ghosts of Christmas;

Behind top-money, big-kennel racers mushing into the last
    two-hundred mile stretch from Unalakleet: wind, blizzard, the
    worst hours like a frozen confetti eternity;

Behind leaders who've smashed themselves again and again battling
    sea ice and tundra coastline, who've vanished and have
    reappeared at last for good at Safety Roadhouse;

Behind the winner singing dogsongs down Front Street, aiming for
    the TV cameras, the chute, the burled-arch finish line, the sledder
    waving to the cheering throngs packed five-deep along sidewalks
    and barroom doorways;

Behind the frostbitten Nomeite from Icy View, Nome Kennel Club
    treasurer, feisty media darling who thrashed predictions by
    trash-talking his inexperienced team across the state, bane of
    animal lovers everywhere, thrice-cited by one ex-wife for non-
    support—sixth-place;

Behind the young Fairbanks dropout, now living alone with his team
    in the woods outside Trapper Creek, top rookie timed in twelve
    days, thirteen hours, nine minutes, forty-two seconds, finishing
    half-past midnight under a juicy full moon—twenty-third place;

Behind the Native woman from the Kenai who fell asleep on the
    runners, dreamt she was part flying grizzly, part grandmother
    eagle, part sunburst salmon, and woke near White Mountain after
    running into a tree stump, tumbling, barely holding on to her
    tangled team—thirtieth place;

Behind the jinxed favorite who suffered catastrophes with moose,
    wolves, food, and had to destroy his leader at Nikolai, another dog
    between Shaktoolik and Koyuk, and one more the day after the
    race—thirty-fourth place;

Behind the wisecracking Ft. Wainwright bachelor lieutenant with the
bad back who stopped in every village along Norton Sound to
receive massage, falling asleep every time mumbling how *my
poor cold little lonely doggy needs a rub*—thirty-eighth place;

Behind the grand old man of the trail who raced together with
daughter and grandson, a trio who knew most everybody at most
every village, so it seemed, and who celebrated Nome by mushing
eighty miles further to Teller—forty-second through forty-fourth
place;

Behind the neckless Frenchman from somewhere in the Alps who
amused competitors at layovers by blowing on a harmonica, until
he wouldn't stop, started blowing louder and louder, and got
busted in the chops by a musher who wanted to sleep—forty-
ninth place;

Behind the Utah rookie who according to doctors was supposed to
have died from breast cancer months before, but refused surgery
and chemo, bought dogs, learned to mush, qualified, raced, and
believed she rode and prayed the illness into remission—fifty-
sixth place;

Behind the group of seven newcomers, which included a husband
and wife from Soldotna, a cowgirl from Wyoming, a Yup'ik mayor
from near Bethel, a bush pilot from Moose Pass, an Anchorage
dentist, and the first African-American woman in the race's
history—fifty-ninth through sixty-fifth place;

Until the last racer, a middle-aged veterinarian from rural Montana,
who struggled haphazardly down Front Street to the serenade of
Nome sirens blaring through new moon darkness, no further
fanfare save for distant stars glittering, the prospect of shower
and shave, a banquet on the house, a trip to the podium to receive
good-natured catcalls, bird whistles, handshakes, hugs, the
traditional red light.

Sports Page

The Anchorage paper is stacked
on the Nome Liquor Store's counter
by five—if the planes can land.
I buy, like the gold miners
and Eskimos who line for booze.

Home, I toss the front page, settle
into the statistical fine print,
a directory of cities and names
that have nothing to do with here.

Nightly, when weather allows, I pore
the news from a forsaken past,
lose myself in warm narcotic.

III

Transistor Radio

One wall removed from my parents'
marriage-long disenchantment, I'd lie
in bed fidgety, too keyed
to sleep, most summer nights saved
from the tension of their terrible
silent accusations by the static
of the black transistor radio
I listened to through the layers
of pillow and pillowcase,
volume on low because my mother
hated her smart-aleck son
to be up late engrossed
in baseball, one more fault
inherited from his father.

When she'd step in to check
if I was still awake, her lips
to my cheek for a lingering
good-night kiss, I'd quickly
click off the box, shift breathing
to just short of death, fake
a twitch or groan, anything
to let her know she'd invaded
depths. As she closed the door,
walked sighing to her room,
I switched on the game, sad
to miss a pitch, the secret
crackly dream re-entered,
an ear to the sheets.

The Champion Mathematician

In the kitchen, Grandma Ruth
scraped congealing fat from a pan,
the stacked pile of china
still undone. Scrambling past,
the grandson slid beneath
the radio cord, picked a noodle
and some crumbs off the floor,
then burst to the den. Spotting him,
Grandpa Dan tossed the sports page
and winked at the father. Turning,
Grandpa Dan shouted, *Quick—*
what's 21 times 37? "777,"
the boy shrieked. The father clicked
the stopwatch. *1.2 seconds,*
he announced. *A new record.*
The mother's eyes shone:
her little Einstein.

Six Iron

One easy June evening, prepping
for the city-wide Father-Son
4th of July Golf Tournament—
my first time on a real course—
I felt like Arnold Palmer charging:
as my scuffed ball knocked
tree trunks on my own half-acre
pitch-and-run, I heard roars,
then imagined me and my dad
on the seventeenth green,
my ten-foot par putt dropping.

At par-five eighteen, needing a bird
to tie, an eagle to win, I'd nod
to my dad, then bust a drive
three-twenty, the ball sitting
right-center of the fairway,
a perfect lie. Next, a big divot
as I'd crack my six iron, cut
the dogleg left. Striding
to the green, I'd find the ball
nine feet from the pin.

In the front yard, I stood over
my Titleist 2, waggled the clubface,
and decided to fly that ball
over the house. Backswing slow
and follow-through long,
I told myself, then stood
still, feeling the warm summer
twilight. A bumblebee hovered.
Then I swung hard, like Arnie would.
Skulled, the shot sailed
through the living room window,
gouged a hole in my mother's

favorite painting, and came to rest—
so I would hear a thousand times—
on the carpet a few feet
from where my father sat drinking
a beer and watching a ball game.

Having looked up too soon,
I had to play that impossible lie.

My Father's Company

Pre-game show on the radio
as we rolled through side-street
Manayunk stop signs, drove
the back way to skip expressway
tie-ups, my father puffed his cigar,
reminded he'd once played center
and defensive tackle, captained
the team his senior year, broken
five bones total, including a thumb
fractured too badly to ever heal.

Top tier, my father's round face,
partially hidden behind binoculars,
delighted at a blitzing linebacker's
late hit, a cornerback's hatchet-like
crack that split flanker from ball.
See that, he'd shout, grinning,
and elbow me, his buddy,
before returning to the customers
who sat beside us, with whom
he talked big numbers and deals.

On the Thirteenth Tee

The first warm April evening,
air so sweet I fell in love
with breathing, I spun
the steering wheel left,
caught 26 East, and thought
of my father, a continent
away, his abiding passion—
the perfect golf swing—
and how summer nights
after dinner he'd take me
to the range on Ridge Pike
where, berating himself
to watch clubhead speed,
he'd slam bucket after bucket,
line shots that soared
past the 250-yard markers,
bounced crazily on rocks,
and rolled to the fence.
One tee away I'd hit my own,
mimicking my dad's grip,
stance, waggle, his pivot,
his too-whippy backswing,
his strike and follow-through.

Arriving at the course,
parking lot and clubhouse
dead, I popped the trunk,
grabbed driver, putter,
three iron, sand wedge,
and a single scuffed ball
from the bag, then changed
into shoes bought last week,
and headed for number one,
a short, easy par-four.
Teeing from the blues,
I whacked a solid drive–

a slight fade—strode
the fairway, lofted
a wedge to the fringe,
two-putted for par.
Making the turn in forty
as a dying sun peeked
through budding maple,
If I sprinted the back,
ignored the blisters,
maybe, just maybe, I'd beat
darkness this round.

Hurried bogeys on dogleg
ten, roadside eleven,
on the par-three twelfth
I buried my three iron
in the bunker to the right
of an elevated, rolling
green. Digging spikes
into the sand, my shoes
sunk ankle-deep, I blasted
the wedge through grit,
and exploded the ball
too strong toward the pin.
I heard the hard knock,
guessed the shot had caromed,
and muttered about a probable
lost ball, the bad lie,
the piss-poor stupid
three iron into the trap,
my tender feet, the idiocy
of this ridiculous game.
After raking the sand,
I climbed the little hill.
Just as I feared—no ball.

The next minutes I trampled
shrubbery and thick grass.
Nothing but an unmarked red

sunset, a spring breeze lost
to search, the year's first
mosquito. About to quit,
I marched to the green
and checked the cup.
There, where it had been—
my bird. Astonished,
I reached in, lifted
the ball, kissed its dimples,
fisted it. Hurrying
to thirteen, I teed low,
peered into the dusk.
A shape staggered from behind
an oak. *Who's that,*
I yelled, squinting,
making out my father's
outline stumbling clubless
up the thirteenth rough.
Dad, I gasped—and ran
limping toward that shadow.

Torn Achilles

Cross-over dribble to lose
his man, then a strong move
to the hoop for a little
two-handed scoop, doing
exactly what he'd practiced
a million times, he felt a pop
at the back of his ankle
over the heel, and fell broken
and groaning in the lane,
this sudden electrocution
of the tendon a burning
like a fuse box of snakes
spitting sparks. And as he lay
writhing on court, a last
scorched wire running
high voltage pain through him,
he recalled his father crouched
over him in the basement
those Sundays before church,
the big fraternity paddle
raised like a baseball bat
as the old man ordered him
to drop pants for a spanking
administered *out of love
and respect*. His father,
frustrated jock, a hard-nosed
bully of a coach, drilled him
to hold every last thing in,
no matter what. The injured son
didn't need a doctor to tell him
the Achilles was shot,
and his crappy father shot it.

Compulsory Fall Sports, Plymouth Academy

From promising fifth-grade
starting halfback, to sixth-grade
second-string quarterback (switched
mid-season to left guard),
to seventh-grade third-string
right tackle, to middle school
substitute soccer goalie,
to high school cross-country
laggard, who struggled up hills
deep into November wishing
only to hit tennis balls,
or to recruit three more
basketball jocks for endless games
of two-on-two, or to find
the finish line of that lousy last
league meet that was run each year
in mud or chill, coach exhorting us
tail-enders to pick up the pace.

Atop Mt. Baker

I reach the summit
late afternoon and stand
for an hour, the sun
at my back, a north wind

rising. Chilled,
I look not to valley
or sky, but the day
I faced that brown bear,

and ran.
That was Alaska,
two summers ago,
a trip that ended

with nothing
worse than a scare.
I'd been lucky.
But I hadn't wanted luck—

only strength, proof
I was an animal
wild and smart
as a grizzly,

an animal unafraid
of meeting another
and taking what was needed
to survive.

Ten thousand feet,
I turn 180 degrees,
gaze above the sun
into a sky

so vast and blue
I stand on Baker
like a weathervane
on a rooftop,

a man taller than any bear.
Then a big gust
almost topples me.
I shiver,

and descend,
picking my way
past ice and rocks
toward camp.

Weight Room

My college freshman self: raw talent
with little strength save a big right forearm
thick from years of hitting millions
of balls. Coach saw a weakling,
sentenced me to the shadows
of the weight room, the clank and grunt,
the huff and muscle of the universal gym.
I didn't even bench press one twenty,
which meant daily reps, extra sessions
on no-practice days. The routine
took me back home, the parental nonsense
that led me to this school. Oh, there was
no escaping. Spraining my knee
on an intramural basketball court—
coming down funny on someone's foot—
I couldn't play for months, lost my slot
the following year to a burly freshman
with a squat body. Coach blamed my lack
of strength. As if brawn made the difference
in groundstroke length, second-serve depth,
the quick first step to the net, a winning
tie-breaker knack. No. My failure was not
this flawed body I was born with.
I was missing the inexplicable.

Sestina for My Father

Father, today we send you home.
How it would please you to see your son
speaking, your friends listening, the sun
shining. A ceremony is a kind of art
and this afternoon the god
of funerals blesses you, father—

all is perfect. I remember when your father,
Siegfried, died. It was at home,
a slow, painful, cancerous dying that God
prolonged. As death neared, you, Arthur, his son,
sat at the bedside and waited. *Art,*
he said, reaching for you. *The sun*

comes for me. I am flying. The sun.
And then he died, Siegfried, your father.
At his funeral you told of his art:
how he left Poland, his father's home,
to come to America; how he fathered a son,
a daughter, a business; how he loved God,

baseball, cigars, his garden. *Oh my God,*
you cried. *How he'd love today, the sun*
out, tomatoes ripening, a game on TV, his son
speaking. Now, twenty-two summers later, father,
amid ripening tomatoes, you, too, are flying home,
and I've been called to practice my art:

the storytelling. Father, my art
saddens me. I cannot play God.
I cannot bring you back. Your home
is now upward, where the sun
rises, where your father,
Siegfried, awaits you, Arthur, his son.

Father, I hope I've been a good son
because being one is a great, great art.
I will always love you, father.
You were a good man. I only hope God
saw you in our yard, crouching in the sun,
thrusting a catcher's mitt behind an improvised home

plate. *Right here, son. A fastball so fast God
won't see. Don't worry. Art'll catch it.* The sun
was shining, father. That was our home.

Tennis Without a Net

Courts finally empty, everyone gone,
we removed a net, Joey and I,
and began cracking groundstrokes like clockwork—
this rallying the sum accumulation
of the millions of balls we'd hit growing up,
balls hit indoors and outdoors, balls hit
on clay, wood, cement, grass, balls hit
moving in, sliding, backpedaling, wrong-footed,
balls hit as dinks, chips, half-volleys,
lobs, balls hit wide, long, on the rise,
over the fence, against a wall, mishit balls,
yellow balls, white balls, orange balls,
spotted balls, dead balls, balls hit right-handed,
left-handed, two-handed, between the legs,
over the shoulder, falling down, diving,
on one knee, on two knees, cramping, bloated,
drunk, exhausted, balls hit in Kalamazoo,
Miami, Chicago, New York, Boston, Atlanta,
balls hit with John McEnroe, with old men,
with girls, balls hit in drizzle, in downpour,
in anger, in spite, balls hit warming up
for 0 and 0 wins and third-set tiebreaker chokes,
balls hit because we loved to, Joey and I,
especially then, twilight, the summer evening
dawdling toward dusk, a couple of lanky
tennis-tanned twenty-year-olds who'd taught
lessons all day, thought to undo a net.
Who knew when the backhands began, backhand
after cross-court backhand, soft floating
underspin backhands, each unerring shot arcing
higher above the imaginary net, deep corner
to deep corner, sky darkening, our shoulders
turned, wrists laid back, long smooth
follow-throughs extending, neither moving
nor seeing, hitting purely by ear, Joey and I,
even after that last perfect ball
disappeared in the unlit July night.

IV

Coyote Poker

When his aces
take the first
hand over my
three kings,
I dangle a toe
which he accepts
with his teeth.

And so on until
I see to beat
my host I must
lay down cards
and eat myself
slowly, beginning
with the mouth.

Tennis Dream

Tense doubles
exchange—several

nervy reflex
volleys. I'm

ball, rackets,
strings, grips,

net, lines,
fence, sky,

clouds, breeze,
the experience

of all
four players

whom I now see
are blindfolded.

Golf Dream

Short par three,
easy swing, divot,

the sphere
perfectly hit,

high in air
to the middle

of green,
but for spin,

wind, slope,
and the ball

rolls slowly at first,
then more quickly

back to front,
slowing in fringe

before disappearing
into the water.

Basketball Dream

I feint left,
cut right,

and steal
the inbounds

pass, make
the lay-up,

feint left,
cut right,

and again steal
the inbounds

pass, make
another lay-up.

I realize then
there is no

scoreboard,
no clock,

no teammates
no opponents,

no official
or unofficial game,

just the ball
I'm to step

in front of,
and steal,

the basket
into which

I'm to lay
the ball.

Boise Dream

We love our corn,
big stalks of summer,

football near. We love
our Blue Thunder

Marching Band,
the drums, our big-play

offense, our strong
and sturdy boys.

Let me tell you
what it means

to live in the green
of the lit, dry

city of trees.
It's our Hollywood.

Americana Boulevard,
where a young man

grows up dreaming,
perhaps to become

lineman, linebacker,
perhaps William Tell

looking at green ash
and sunset maple,

the brown hills
over and over,

loving our corn
over and over,

our prettiest girls
leading the cheers.

Football Dream

I break through
the line of scrimmage

untouched. I'm not
tripped up. I'm

in motion—a snap
and I take

the hand-off,
break through

the line of scrimmage
untouched. I'm not

tripped up.
I'm the man

in motion—a snap
and I take

the hand-off,
break through.

Baseball Dream

Between shortstop
and third base

a hole
a half mile

deep. Sharply
hit grounders

don't reach
left field

and vanish.
Occasionally

baserunners, too,
disappear mid-

stride never
to be seen again.

The Decathlete's Dream

I

Stretch for a good hour.
An eleven second sprint.
That's the way to start.

II

No ordinary
uncoiling. It's a fast dance,
releasing discus.

III

A different sprint—
run hard, plant the pole harder.
Get up and over.

IV

You run once again,
this time with spear. You let go,
flinging with a shout.

V

Quick sprint that's double,
triple, quadruple. Each breath
deep work. Wobbly legs.

VI

Day two, more stretching.
Then hurdle, hurdle, hurdle,
hurdle. Churn and churn.

VII

Yet another sprint,
then the take-off. Imagine
thin air. Fly further.

VIII

Spin, push, grunt. Heavy
iron flies through air. Not quite
a birthing, but close.

IX

This, too, is about
timing: curved approach, take-off,
new angle and flop

X

Run until you can't.
Four hard minutes or more. Run.
If it hurts, you've won.

Supermoon Dream

Waves smash
against the black rock
the lighthouse sits on.

Night swells. High tide,
and he walks what beach
remains beneath cliff,

kicking a rag of kelp
stuck to his boots.
He steps into the surf,

submerging both feet.
The next waves roll,
wash, ebb, leaving

the bottom of his wetsuit
caked. He paddles
hard, then turns, waits,

climbs atop board,
then leans, letting
a big one catch.

Inside soaked roar,
he rides dark water
to shoreline.

Colin Kaepernick's Dream

Martin Luther King Day
parade, I'm in front

with Tommie Smith,
John Carlos, Muhammad Ali,

Arthur Ashe, Curt Flood,
Kareem Abdul Jabbar,

Jackie Robinson, LeBron James,
Satchel Paige, Connie Hawkins,

Marlin Briscoe, Joe Gilliam,
Doug Williams, Warren Moon.

Behind us, hundreds
of brothers and sisters

of all sizes, shapes,
and shades. Thousands;

no, millions. We fill
every road into and out of

Washington D.C..
We kneel and pray.

The Fan's Dream

The ref
whistles me
for delay
of game.
I protest—

I'm sitting
in the third row
and the game
isn't supposed
to start

for a half hour.
I'm given
two technicals
and am tossed
from building.

Editorial

There's a brilliance
to the deviance

of doctors and coaches
who approach

the teen and pre-teen
talent. How they're seen

as outstanding
role models, treating

and teaching. Clever
how you'd never

suspect a mess
so obvious

yet subtle—
cuddles

born in the cuddlers' own
sorry boyhood homes.

These grown men's dreams,
alas, come with the game—

so unseemly,
so criminal, so creepy.

The Blackjack Dream

He's dealt a 3 in the hole,
a 9 showing. Hit me,
he says. She flips him

another 9. I stick—21, he says.
But the dealer, a birthmark
on her cheekbone, painted fingernails,

slides one more card, a red
6. She cackles. The two 9's
somersault one and a half times:

the spun numbers winning him
                        losing him
                waking him.

V

Twin Killing

It looks so easy, a quick 6-4-3
double-play, two-hopper to short, underhand
feed to the pivoting second-baseman
who fires to first. It looks so easy,
though it's not. To field the ball cleanly
and efficiently is an art. Understand
the teamwork in getting a sliding lead man—
spikes flying—and sidestepping injury
to complete the relay. The umpire's hand
signals out as the first baseman's long stretch
beats the runner's last big stride to the bag.
The 6-4-3 double-play. A casual fan
never will comprehend the beauty. Such
is the game's stark, sudden, graceful zig-zag.

Swimmer as Our Adolescent God

Every morning for how many long years
he wakes at 5, is driven to the pool
for practice laps. Saturdays, Sundays, school
days, holidays, summer days. His mom swears
he's growing fins. His cheerleader girlfriend fears
an addiction to chlorine. First high-school dual
meet he sets state records, three strokes. A mule
for water, as a frosh he beat seniors
who've earned college scholarships. Sophomore
year, his coach says he's splashing on the door
of national teams, owns Olympic speed—
has a man's body, a champion's need.
Like Achilles, down to the heel. The boy
quits at sixteen to sleep in, goof off, annoy.

On Tour

4-5, 30-40, set point against,
you barely miss with the big flat first serve.
Experience says best to summon nerve,
slow things down, ignore the circumstance,
just spin the ball deep to the backhand. You sense
he'll run around to crack a forehand, a blur
skipping by. You want to throw him a curve,
a hard slice down the middle. You're tensed,
going for the ace. Your opponent sees
your shift. Maybe it's a guess. He doesn't budge,
decides to play it straight. Everybody freeze:
tennis at this high level is a grudge
match in guts. The best are best for making
like cats. The rest? Mice for the taking.

Johnny Football

You make the stadium all electric,
wicked big-play freak of a quarterback,
sneaky scrambler, pass-happy maniac
shotgun trickster: quick huddle, snap, a slick
fake to fullback, quick downfield look, a quick
flick to wideout in the flat. Or else back
a few steps, the pocket. You have that knack
to make tacklers miss, to precisely pick
apart a weak defense. Johnny Football,
campus hero, freshman Heisman winner,
one-part regular Kerrville Joe who's all
yes sir and yes ma'am, one-part steak dinner
in a hip new nightclub with wine and girls,
one-part Aggie set to hot-wire the world.

The Professional

You walk in the trap, spot the buried lie,
and think this so true of your not-so-bright
life striking a five iron that felt right,
watching it rise lazy in the air, high
and straight, maybe a slight fade, a tad shy
perhaps. Or does the wind suddenly fight,
a quick gust, the saddest of golf sights—
ball on way to green flies just short and dies
in the sand. Entering that bunker, you view
a lump, your dismal and familiar you.
Taking your stance, you do your job—a dig
in with your spikes, the wedge well-gripped, a big
swing, contact behind, letting the sand lift
the ball. Your life's work. No wonder you're miffed.

PK4

Big brain sport: sixty-four black-and-white squares
that encompass more. It's war, for godsakes.
War of nerve, of stamina, war that takes
strategy and clock. Always there are layers
within layers. Quick thrusts, quirky feints, puny dares
that trap. No shallow scrimmaging here. Fakes
quickly lose themselves in confusion. Snakes
of dream logic. Out of chaos, strength. There's
room for psychology, genius; there's a room
to smoke. It's a ball field for ornery
mathematicians, a metaphor for hate.
Watch the humans play computers. Assume
the simpleton is two moves slow. Victory
involves sacrifice, insight, study, wait.

The Dreamer Steps Out Into the World

So much easier in an empty gym
to bounce the ball three times, barely aim, swish
one free throw, the next, and the next. You wish
you could save these shots, pack them in a slim
suitcase, get fouled, take them out, shoot, no rim,
clean, calmly ice games by sinking the pair. Swish.
Swish. Mr. Ninety-three per cent. You wish
you could bottle it. This touch. This feel. Trim
everything extraneous. No ball, no
foul line, no basket, no court, no free throw,
no history. Just the perfect present,
the world naturally messy, silent,
talky. You walk light as air, your own king,
queen, country. Acting, reacting, breathing.

The Other Game

Occasionally in this life, if we put
in the hard practice time, we'll rise—or fall—
for a day, week, or more into what's called
the zone. The sport inside the sport. It's what
we work toward—sinking a short birdie putt
to close a match; moving without the ball
to score forty after perfect feeds; all
those sliders looking like slow brown coconuts
as we take a home-run cut at the plate,
connect, feel the ball fly off the bat,
begin our trot. We ask how to duplicate
these feats. Answer: We can't. They're the cat
tempting us to try again, just in case.
The zone comes as logically as love. Or grace.

The Horses

Take five dollars, amble to an open window,
and put the money on the seven horse.
Back at your seat, watching the race, of course
you've bought an interest as you follow
your boy along the far turn. *Go Go Go,*
you yell, willing your jockey to use more force,
not get boxed. Money is hardly the source
of evil. Here at the track it's the dough
that makes every deadbeat dream. Five dollars—
and you're part owner, part rider, part nag.
You've earned the right to moan, curse, holler,
jump up and down, beam, float, laugh. Or else sag
at a photo-finish loss. A cheap date.
Though I advise you leave early, come late.

Home Team Blown Out

First quarter: seventy-yard flea-flicker
for six quick points on the opening drive.
Three and out, then a punt, all shuck and jive
as the returner makes seven tacklers
look stupid. Next, a blitzing linebacker
sacks fumbling scrambler on the thirty-five—
big right end scoops pigskin, rumbles, then dives
untouched into the end zone. Second quarter:
our all-star wide-out lies crumpled at midfield,
gets carried off on a stretcher. Half-time,
cheerleaders bump, grind, somersault, let loose
with the roars. Fifty-thousand fans wink, peeled
to their favorite girls Third quarter: dine
on more bratwurst, beer. Down thirty, the boos.

Off-Season

End of the year, first a soak, then a beer,
then board the team bus, then nap in the airplane
home. No practice, no meetings, no more games—
or painkillers!–until pre-season, a mere
four months away. One trick is to appear
productive. Another is to sleep. Retain
a sense of humor. Unclog the storm drain.
Buy the wife a bracelet. Mull the career.
Buy the kids new computers. Go play golf.
Take that one fattening extra nibble,
lunch and dinner. Soon there's this need to wolf
homemade pie and Haagen-Dazs pints. Trouble
lurks on a scale not in any bathroom.
Watch yourself, athlete. Bust follows boom.

LeBron

21st century he-man specimen,
all-time pick for raw power plus speed.
Sneaky-quick ball handler. Can rebound, feed,
score, play shut-down D. Teammate, citizen,
hardwood icon. Off season regimen:
life at the gym. Recipe to succeed:
endless practice, and a pledge against greed—
four years he shared the court with a best friend.
Recognized in Greece, India, China,
face and game well-known to Obama.
Physical gifts and singular talent:
MVP, league champ, Olympic gold. It meant
leaving hometown Akron for Miami.
Then the return in behalf of family.

After the Fifteenth Round

The body was found in the bedroom,
wrapped in a sheet. My athletic old man,
former three-sport letterman, who still ran
triathlons into his seventies. Soon,
the obituary, the funeral. Then comes
the burial. Golfing last month, the old man
matched his age. Bowling last week, the old man
rolled a smooth, one-sixty. Now he's gone,
though the force remains. Already stories
about this, his last race, almost outpacing
death, until he slipped. Lack of energy
wasn't it. Just parts breaking. No worries,
at least not what you'd expect. That crazy
old jock. He's shadowboxing now, missing me.

Bunker

for Pete and family

Like a movie, what happened after dad
died. His wish: to have his ashes buried
in the same sand trap as his wife, Viv. We'd
expected his death. But still. This was dad.
Our extraordinary dad. The old man had
feared a last long illness, hated he'd need
to burden others, didn't want to bleed,
just hold that active self that never had
to end. Dad, it hasn't. We kids journey
to your home course, Singing Hills Country Club,
draw straws. Long straw takes the shovel. Short straw,
the ashes. Playing the eighteen holes, we
replay your life—and ours. This golf club
is tribal owned. We follow your law.

26.2

After all the training, all the pain,
you line up with several hundred others.
The first miles are easy. We're all brothers
and sisters, you think, happy to sustain
this early pace. Then the slight hamstring strain
or calf spasm. The blister. Grandmothers,
too, curse each new step. Marathoners
treat discomfort as cornfields do rain.
Necessary clouds. Breaks from dry horizon
and hill. Asphalt, tall grass, crud. A frozen
prairie melts. Rainbow's gate. Little distance
to finish now. Each stride like a high fence
to climb, straddle, jump. Twenty-six mile runs,
like any journey, have a thousand destinations.

Sportswriter

The swirl of computer, deadline, pressbox
makes language almost too stiff for end zone
celebrations, slam dunks, the one-on-one
duels, the games within games, how a kid knocks
on the bench for years, gets a chance, then rocks
the league, slumps, then like that is let go, gone,
next stop Paducah, Ames, Alpena, Trenton,
or else suit and tie, dark shoes, darker socks,
a place in the town where he almost made it.
Like the young sportswriter, who loves the job
of watching and reporting, but had a dream
of competing. Who now wrestles each edit,
executes tight little tales about Bob,
Sam, Julius, and the rest of the home team.

VI

The Shamanism of Baseball

Where white man with stick aims at ball
        thrown by gloved man on mound
        to gloved masked man crouched
        behind whisked five-sided plate

where man in dugout signals to man
        in box who signals to man with stick
        to take, sacrifice, swing away

where men in black pronounce run, walk,
        balk, strike, steal, foul, out, OUT!

where millions sit motionless, entranced
        by timelessness that can be clocked
        in two or three hours, more or less

Duel

The pitcher winds.
A fastball
that climbs.
Swing. Foul ball.

A fastball
just outside.
Swing. Foul ball.
The pitcher strides—

just outside.
Swing. Foul ball.
The pitcher strides.
Foul ball.

Swing. Foul ball.
He's protecting the plate.
Foul ball.
A long at bat,

protecting the plate.
Again foul ball.
A long at bat.
Again foul ball.

Again foul ball.
Catcher opens his mitt.
Again foul ball.
Nothing to hit.

Catcher opens his mitt.
Again foul ball.
Nothing to hit.
A fastball—

again foul ball. A fastball
that climbs.
A fastball. Foul ball.
The pitcher winds.

3 and 2 Count, Runner on First, Two Out

When the pitcher
has got to come in,

the good ones know
to work the batter

by stepping off
the mound, looking long

to first, spitting,
raising pitching hand

to the bill of the cap,
then rubbing the ball

a second. Toeing
the rubber, going

into the stretch,
looking again at first,

and again, why not throw low
and just outside.

Why shouldn't
the hungry hitter bite?

The Wild Ones

More effective than sly pitchers shrewdly
changing speeds, nibbling the outside corner,
the wild ones don't ever let poor batters
get comfortable. Each throw is duly
fastball, fastball, fastball, maybe a crude
slider, the ball maybe somewhere over
the plate, 97 miles per hour.
The lack of control is just filthy rude.
Isn't this how all of us face the day?
Either pitcher with the most wicked stuff
without the talent to exercise it,
or hitter with weak stick, who has to pray
an errant toss doesn't crack a skull. Tough
shit, that's our life: we go out and wing it.

That's What They Pay Him For

Tough call—
Have Duvall take? Or give him the green light?
But that's baseball,

the manager thinks, two ball
count. Duvall looks kinda tight.
Tough call—

the lefty's tiring: Goddamn slumping Duvall.
Two on, two out, need a run. Christ,
but that's baseball—

bet the house on a fastball
down the pipe. Take or green light?
Tough call.

The manager tugs his cap, pulls
an ear, scratches his white
butt. That's baseball—

gotta let that joker Duvall
swing away. That's right.
Tough call.
But that's baseball.

Four-Game Dog-Day Series

Mid-August, more of the same
for the Angels and Sox.
Another meaningless game

but for the stats, the names
in the boxscore. Look at the clock—
mid-August, more of the same

uninspired play. Who can blame
fans for flinging verbal rocks.
Another meaningless game

between last-place teams—lame
pitching, sick fielding, spoiled jocks.
Mid-August, more of the same

sad drama. The owners claim
record losses. The players trade stocks.
Another meaningless game

on Chicago's South Side. A shame.
Where's old Nellie Fox?
Mid-August, more of the same.
Another meaningless game.

Denny

Whatever happened to Denny McLain,
who owned baseball for a season?
31 wins, a fighter's heart, a brain

fueled by Pepsi. At his best, a game
and gutsy righty, pride of Michigan.
Whatever happened to Denny McLain

post-sport? Crazy weight gain,
racketeering, incarceration.
31 wins, a flighty art, a brain

attracted to alternative fame,
sly gambler bent on self-destruction.
Whatever happened to Denny McLain,

wily fastballer, strong-armed high-octane
maestro on mound and organ?
31 wins? 31 mighty starts, a brain

unsuited for the fast far lane.
Hero? Not his chosen profession.
Whatever happened to Denny McLain?
31 wins delight a part of our brain.

Baseball Hall of Fame

Cooperstown honors Jimmie Foxx.
I honor odd memories—
swept pitcher's mound and batter's box

between innings, a crafty Greg Maddux
working out of a jam against the Phillies.
Cooperstown honors Jimmie Foxx.

I honor the Bill Lee Red Sox,
the Jamie Moyer Mariners, Dock Ellis on LSD,
swept pitcher's mound and batter's box—

Giants and A's, Cubs and White Sox,
Jackie Robinson winning a World Series.
Cooperstown honors Jimmie Foxx,

Babe Ruth, Joe DiMaggio, Ted Williams, Bobby Cox.
I honor Luis Tiant, Dick Allen, Tommy Agee,
swept pitcher's mound and batter's box,

Chris Short holding Maury Wills or Lou Brock
on first, Jim Kaat versus Carl Yastrzemski.
Cooperstown honors Jimmie Foxx.
I honor swept pitcher's mound and batter's box.

Number 6

Al Kaline, Mr.Tiger, three easy
syllables to help long-time Detroit fans
hark back to the years of dream Motown bands:
The Temptations, Four Tops, Supremes. Breezy
TV days of Ed Sullivan, Ozzie
and Harriet, Green Acres, Gunsmoke. Cans
of soup, compliments of Andy Warhol. Brands
of cigarettes: Old Gold, Viceroy, Lucky
Strike. Al Kaline, 3,000 hits, home run
threat, rifle arm in right, little flair or flash,
just Hall of Fame teammate. So many seasons
batting third between McAuliffe and Cash.
Tiger arms? Think Lary, McLain, Lolich.
Past Number 6, the summer of Fidrych.

Injured List

Off the funny bone, where tendon
joins muscle, the sporadic
debilitating pain demands
tight attention, a fit metaphor
for a reliever who can't

loosen up, though with each ache
he gently tunnels that way,
listens like a doctor—his desire
for wholeness like a stethoscope
to the joint—and notes

the truth revealed inside.
His right elbow, now stuck,
seems to have been drafted
to serve a tour in a country
devoid of sport,

a blighted zone so reminiscent
of forgotten childhood trauma
that the body, now closed
to normal days, must have opened
the past in order to heal

a man buried under his weight.
Soon, when his family wars lift
and full use of the arm returns,
this, too, will pass as history,
a lesson to call up, and learn from.

Imaginary St. Louisan

My father, Albert, was called Archie,
or Arch, my father, baseball-loving,
football-following Philadelphian,
a businessman who should have lived
in St. Louis. Instead, an imaginary
St. Louisan, an imaginary giant
Cardinal fan, who when he answered to Arch
could have spent his last years
as a switch-hitter, one day mimicking
Musial, the next day Pujols, swinging
an imaginary bat, hitting an imaginary
ball, pointing happily east at his imaginary
blast. Arch, where the imaginary St. Louisan
might have found his furthest fence,
before crossing that river home.

VII

With the Poet Who's Been Anthologized Everywhere

He wanted help on his backhand approach
so I hit some, told him not to run through the shot,
but to stop, turn, keep the weight
on the front foot. The poet got it—
*so it's like skiing: you let the mountain
do the work*, he said—and we continued
to backhand volleys, overheads, serves.
Then he asked to play points. Stretching,
running like a much younger man, the poet
reached balls he shouldn't have,
once making me sprint the width
of the court where I passed him
with a topspin cross-court backhand
after he slid a perfect forehand approach
down-the-line. Seeing his scowl—
he'd thought his shot unreturnable
I maneuvered the ball on the next point
so he hit another one good and deep.
This time I didn't hit quite so hard,
the poet was leaning right, and he angled
away the backhand volley. *Good lesson*,
he said later, huffing, as we shook hands
at the net. *Now how much did you say?*
Waving him off, I said: *I write poems.*

For a second he sized me up like a doctor,
then went to his wallet. *How much
did you say? Forty?*

Laying two twenties in my palm,
the poet snarled: *Watch out for the I.R.S.—
the government eats us.*

1971 National Junior and Boys, Kalamazoo

Opening Sunday I marveled
how the top-seeded junior,
Vitas Gerulaitis, demolished
a big hitter from Ohio
in less than fifty minutes,
the favorite wowing the crowd
with his pure and cool
boyish joy, a kid
who could bang the hell
out of a tennis ball,
then race the court to retrieve
anything, clipping lines
with flick cross-court forehands,
deep down-the-line backhands,
topspin lobs, his quick grin
celebrating the genius
and flair fairly bursting beneath
an unruly blond mop of hair.

Monday afternoon, a back court,
I went out and lost
my own first round match,
a workaday straight-setter
to a burly lefty from Tampa
whose game I never figured.
If only I had the speed,
skill, and luck of Gerulaitis,
I moaned for days afterwards,
me, the callow and gangly slowpoke
from suburban Philadelphia
who served hard, returned well,
could hit any shot,
but didn't have a clue
that to compete at this level
a player needed a will
to go with the verve.

Tennis Made Easy

Three words on an old business card,
ash of once-held ambitions
to write advertising, coach a sport,
simplify hard practice. From Boston
to Chapel Hill to Seattle to Fairbanks
(where two summers I was farthest north
tennis pro in the U.S.) to Juneau,
soggy, soppy end of the line.
By then I'd completed grad school,
learned narrative tricks, felt the teaching
of story and form a more personal
and rewarding calling than backhands.

Nearly five years since I last stood
at a net, feeding hoppers of balls
to groups of eager kids reminding me
of that cocky twelve-year-old self
who found a haven on the baseline
serving and returning serve,
cracking deep top-spinning forehands
that pinned opponents to the fence,
who finished off points with an approach
and volley. That's the boy I've lost,
the lanky winner with the long
flowing follow-through, aiming at sky.

College Sweethearts

For two years the couple crossed
the main quad arm-in-arm,
smug and unsmiling en route
to 10 o'clock class, he the tall
handsome tennis team captain
who lost his serve in the clutch,
she an also-ran sprint freestyler,
a scholarship washout.

When the full-length mirror
revealed two overmatched jocks
struggling in sports
that no longer fit, they cracked
the glass with twin fists, fixed
aim on each other, a bloody fight
won in an out-of-town motel's
groaning king-sized bed.

Pamplona Trip: The Matador

Across from me, you,
bull, rush the ring.
I swirl my cape,

bait back.
Nostrils flaring,
you snort.

When you paw at dirt,
bellowing, I unsheathe
my sword, knowing

your drooping ears,
your brutish heart,
live for my hand speed,

my guile.
When you lunge,
I slay.

Squatting over you,
I slice off your ears
because I need them.

Rodeo Vet

Thrown, then kicked
by a bucking roan,
the rodeo vet lay
crumpled in dirt,
brackish fluids oozing
from a ruined body,
the drained blond face
an albino mask.
As one clown shooed
the bronc so others could
lift the downed rider
onto a stretcher,
over the loudspeaker
an announcer requested
all bareback entries
to gather at the chute.
The rodeo vet, gurgling
on vomit, struggled to rise
until his cowboy heart
collapsed, squeezed
by the rope's last pull.

City League

Predictable in unpredictability,
some are jocks straining waistline
to waistline against wifely cooking
and clock. The rest: divorced shooters,
hapless board men, bachelor actors,
baseline losers, turnover-prone boozers
who happen to own or manage
the sponsoring restaurant or bar.
Ah, but for slow, stocky guards
to whip behind-the-back passes
into stands, redeeming themselves
by caroming three-pointers off glass,
nodding their heads, playground casual
as they backpedal, as if they'd called bank.
Clumsy big men to flick bricks that swish.
The half to find one ref tap dancing beside
home team bench or scorer's table, shmoozing.
His partner out in the parking lot, smoking.

NBA Coach

Part psychologist, part strategist,
it takes a certain kind of man,
a hardwood Jesus Christ,

to endure the challenges and persist.
It's insufferable work. He does what he can,
part psychologist, part strategist,

juggler of line-up, time-out, big-ego weirdness.
Popovich, Kerr, Carlisle, McMillan,
each a hardwood Jesus Christ

or Jungian therapist
for wing, point guard, big man.
Part psychologist, part strategist,

survivor of 82 games of missed
assignments, blown calls, loudmouth fans.
A hardwood Jesus Christ

who braves every last mile and twist
from LAX to Madison Square Garden.
Part psychologist, part strategist
of hardwood. Then the playoffs. Jesus Christ.

Tennis Parent: The Finals

At courtside he sits in the car watching
his lefthanded twelve-year-old spin
a second serve to the forehand corner,
crack a backhand approach down-the-line
for a winner. It's five games to three,
favor of his son, third set. Preparing
to return serve now, he fidgets and kicks
dirt on the baseline, a young McEnroe,
five foot shadow lengthening, an autumn sun.

He returns to the poetry he's holding—Roethke.
Fish, flower, seed, dust: his language
a language of temporary order,
his rhythm the rhythm of a man playing
tennis. He shuts his eyes, sees the red clay
his dad taught him on. A scrapper,
the old man hit hard, moved well, made him
earn every point. *Dad*. The passenger door
opens. His son climbs in, the victor.

Inner Life of a Race Car Driver

Yesterday's sports: another
two hundred plus mph crash
into a wall, an auto
on fire, a racer hospitalized
in stable condition with fractured
pelvis and knee, first degree
burns to the hands. Faced
with months to heal,
this Formula One casualty
must lay cracked and blistered,
the boredom only broken
by replay of that near-fatal
skid and spin, the repair
to bone, skin, soul,
a spirit that leaves sickbed
to at last acknowledge the edge:
a push to new top speeds
four hundred horsepower
roaring toward forgiveness.

Cyclists

I

Beneath an indecipherable
sky, a cyclist pedals
north uphill toward lake.

II

A cyclist spills turning
a corner, worn ice
smooth as a tooth.

III

No hand on handlebar,
a cyclist munching an apple
rides the center stripe.

IV

Half past midnight,
town streetlights miles back,
a cyclist clicks to tenth.

V

Truck, rock, dog, hole,
glare, tar, dust, glass,
a windblown cyclist weaves all.

Iron Men

So they've succumbed
to the inevitable

creak and strain
of chronic joint pains—

trick elbows and ankles,
repetitions

that wear down psyches
and knees—or fallen

to the more acute
freak career-enders.

What's next? Athletes
who run wind sprints

with spirit, whose eyes
are the ball in play,

find the greatest sport
begins at home, nightly,

retiring into dream,
tight beside wife.

We All Swim Away

Morning, the burnt head lifts from water
to breathe. Bright arms pull toward earth.
Wind-borne legs flutter-kick clouds, splashing
white. All day one stroke. Evening, the head,
catching fire, drops in darkening pool.

Who is not swimming: The father riding
his horse across a frozen field, a moonless
November sunset? The mother sitting alone,
lap full of gray wool, knitting a sweater
for a son who shuns her? The man and wife

entwined, hair stringy, bodies slick
from sex? The child crawling upstairs, giggling,
reaching the top, stumbling a few steps
before falling? The sun cupping the sky,
a steady ball on the blue horizon?

Who is not swimming? To wake is to burst
with fingers knifed, toes curled, back muscles
arched and rippling: a butterfly. To rise
is to flutter, orange and black ascending,
a monarch, striped wings shining as they beat.

Natural History

They're playing ping-pong, Satan and God.
Sun and moon belong to God, of course,

then to Satan, then to God, to Satan,
to God. As do the grasses, the creatures,

the sports. And you and I, we're crammed
tight inside the spinning white ball

that gets whacked, whacked, whacked,
faster and faster, the masters' master.

CPSIA information can be obtained
at www.ICGtesting.com
Printed in the USA
BVHW032058170220
572477BV00005B/10